THE AGE
OF
OLIVE TREES

Haia Mohammed

Out-Spoken Press
London

Published by Out-Spoken Press,
PO Box 78744
London, N11 9FG

First edition published 2025
ISBN: 978-1-0686712-5-8

Typeset in Futura and Adobe Caslon
Design by Patricia Ferguson
Printed and bound by Print Resources

Out-Spoken Press is supported using public funding by the National
Lottery through Arts Council England.

Supported using public funding by
ARTS COUNCIL
ENGLAND
LOTTERY FUNDED

THE AGE OF OLIVE TREES

CONTENTS

to all those with stubborn eyes
like the olive tree who refuses to uproot
never stop your defiance

FOREWORD

When I first encountered Haia's words I knew I had encountered a true poet. Unflinchingly, she speaks the difficult truth whilst retaining a fierce tenderness, wisdom and startling poetic.

I have had the honour of working with Haia with an urgency since the temporary ceasefire was broken, gathering and shaping together a body of work – to which this pamphlet is a window – all whilst she remains displaced in Gaza and continues to endure, and to write, in the midst of the ongoing genocide.

Recently someone said to me that the truest poems travel the shortest distance from the pen to the heart.

> *Look at the universe, look closely, and ponder...*
> *Isn't it magnificent? All of it is made for you.*
> *Do you still think you are nothing?*
> *What strength do you have within that you*
> *continue to bury and ignore?*

These poems are small miracles born in the midst of unimaginable circumstance. The borders are currently closed. All aid has been refused entry. The genocide continues whilst the people of the world protest and global powers remain complicit.

Out-Spoken Press's enduring support of the poet and commitment to publishing this swiftly with all proceeds going to the poet and her family, my capacity to draw Haia's words together as a fellow poet and friend, to honour her essence and intention while she continues to resist and persist, and our collective intention to refuse the systematic erasure of Palestinian voice and art, demonstrate the collaborative and revolutionary ways in which art can and should function in these genocidal times

Art should hold us accountable and dignify us in tangible and intangible ways.

Art must function not appease.

We are in a time when even language is suffering fatigue. In the UK, our media, governments and art institutions speak of neutrality or refuse language its right to true meaning altogether.

Haia's words stand in stark defiance and soar with the necessity of imaginative possibility. Her poems concisely and precisely hold us to account with their clarity of thought and a complete refusal of self-pity. She speaks to ordinary love in the most devastatingly extraordinary of circumstances – something no young person should ever have to do. She communes with the past, the present and the future of her people and her homeland. Haia's poems move you from belief to certainty that a better world is within reach because her work lives in it- galvanising the beauty & power of language and flying it in the face of despair.

The Polish poet Czesław Miłosz wrote, 'What is poetry which does not save / Nations or people?'

When I asked Haia what poetry means to her she said, 'It is the language through which I speak to kindred spirits unrestricted by borders. It's my means of resistance; my voice that transcends limitations.'

I hope these poems unearth and revive you. I hope they support you to transcend your own limitations as they continue to do for me. I hope you are emboldened and grow braver for inhabiting them a while.

Palestine is and will be free. Haia's words stand as testament to it.

—Sunnah Khan,
April 2025

I do not fear death, rather, I fear life.

RAMADAN

the earth
will   grow   stifling
narrow   but the seven heavens
will open
wide   on a moon
lit night
when it reaches   its fullness
mid-month

pause to listen –

in its silence   you may hear
words   the world could   never
grant   you
and in its completion

you   may   find

your own

HOW DO YOU FIND THE WAY TO MY HOMELAND?

I carry a backpack through life / moving from place to place to escape / somehow I remain attached to my land / when I return to the tent at night I pass a lady cooking on a clay oven / the irresistible food fills the air / I say to her *what a wonderful smell* / she replies *please come my daughter* / she doesn't know me / I don't know her / I know that this food isn't even enough for her family / this is inevitable in war / she invites me in / calls me her daughter / I realise this is my homeland's true path / when there's only one loaf of bread left for two days no one touches it / despite everyone starving / until my mother divides it among us / then I know I'm on the right path / whatever dish she prepares she sends to her neighbours / they do the same / so no one sleeps hungry / when you go to offer condolences for their martyred children / you find yourself / being comforted instead by their immense patience / faith / strength / walking through streets / you see people sweeping / organising remnants of their homes / others living in a remaining room / their destroyed house / a man sitting on his balcony chair / in the rubble / having breakfast / when you go to buy something / the seller tells you *pay what you can, if you can't pay, don't* / then you realise who the true owners of the land are /

نحن الباقون

كبرتُ في ظلِّ زيتونةٍ غرسَها جدي بيديه المُتعبتين،
وسقاها من عرقِ أبي الجبين وملح الحكايات،
وأنا اليومُ أحرسُها كأني أحرسُ الوطن.
شجر الزيتون في بلادي ينطق بالحق،
أعمارُه تمتدُّ في التربة أعمقَ من آثار الغزاة،
وأغصانُه تشهدُ:
نحن الباقون...نحن وهم الزائلون.

5

THE LIVING MARTYR

I was   destined to face death   from the first day   October 7th
my mother insisted we leave   the house   displaced   to my brother's
my family and I determined   to stay   didn't want to evacuate or abandon
our home   *I told her if we are to die, then let it be here*   we stood
firm   in our refusal   my brother came   pleading for us to leave   after his
urging   it was my mother   who decided   we should evacuate
to his house   a few days later the entire area around us was was obliterated
a fierce ring of fire   my room   most heavily damaged   a massive
concrete   pillar   fell   onto my bed   where I had just been
sleeping   it was after that my family started calling me   *the living martyr*

I AM GAZA, I AM HAIA

Daughter of a land that cannot be defeated
a voice of a sky that never betrays

I'm the blood that flows through its streets
the pulse beneath the rubble that never ceases

every day my eyes witness death but my heart
knows only life

I carry on my shoulders the pain of a nation
and on my lips the voice of defiance

I'm the story the world cannot forget.
the sword that will not break the soul

to the world I will not ask you to save me
I will not seek your pity

In the face of my strength you will feel powerless
I am Haia – daughter of Gaza

my voice is louder than any bomb
my spirit deeper than any wound.

91 DAYS

After 91 days of war I've become someone else.
I believe there's an entire world inside me –
happiness, love, strength – I just need to search
within myself to find what I want.

I don't need anything from the fake external world.
I realise surrendering doesn't suit me nor do I fit in it.
We were created in the battlefield of life to be first-class
warriors.

Today, I realise that the people of Gaza are different
perhaps created from a special clay with stubborn eyes
a heart I can't quite describe, but who could endure
living through what the people of Gaza experience?

War taught me. I was raised by it once again. Learning
not to attach myself to anything, no matter what it is.
I possess now nothing except my backpack. I learned
how not to be attached to things, places or memories.

I learned how a person can offer their soul in the face
of death without hesitation and leave everything behind.
I remember asking my grandparents how life was when
there was occupation in Gaza –

they would tell us stories that seemed more like fiction
today I realise the truth in those stories. I used to wonder
how our ancestors lived. I'd ask my grandmother and she'd
say how they ate, cooked and moved, I'd be amazed.

Today Grandma I live your life, I've become an engineer in fire
feeding, work part-time handwashing clothes…
Honestly the people of Gaza don't need to study history
they live it.

THE SEA CALLS ME

I am a part of this water part of this vastness part of this mystery I am a part
of this turbulence and calm when I stand before the sea it's as if I see my pieces together
  I feel strong. Defiant. Free. Just like these waves I step forward and dive
into the depths of a distant horizon. I see my spirit scatter like foam
only to return merging with every ebb and flow I move
press feet upon sand the earth teaches me the meaning of steadfastness
at the same time I rise with the waves soaring I return as I am. Unbounded.
Unchained. I listen. Hear my heart's echo in the surge. The sea calls me
I accept becoming part of its expanse.

INSTRUCTIONS ON HOW TO LIVE THROUGH A GENOCIDE

1. Embrace the pain and be grateful that it has befallen you. Before this pain, you were one person, and through it you have become someone else, filled with wisdom and maturity. This pain has shaped you.

2. Be grateful for the small blessings, starting with a healthy body, a sip of water, a plate of food, the vast sky around you the white clouds and the birds remind you of freedom the sea, the stars and again white.

3. What happened in the past happened and ended. You live today and the future is ahead, the past is a finished story.

4. Try singing and dancing under the moonlight, smiling at the sky, shouting with the sea, racing waves, or remembering those things you did in your childhood, laughing like never before.

5. Live your day as if it's your last because you're only alive now. Don't dwell on past nightmares or fear the future because they are things you don't possess. Value what you have and make it yours.

6. Plant a tree, take care of it and watch it grow. A feeling indescribable.

7. Run through the rain and breathe.

8. Share your pain with a close friend or family member, but choose the right person and distribute it on two shoulders instead of one.

9. Let your self-confidence soar with the birds. You are not an ordinary person; you have faced all the pain alone and are still here. What strength lies within you? No one knows your story don't let them judge. Rise and place the remaining pieces in their spots. Show them who you are.

10. In the middle of the night, when everyone is asleep, rise to pray and ask for what you want and need. He is here, in the first sky, closer to you than your jugular vein, listening and answering your prayers.

11. *'Perhaps He gave you and withheld from you, and perhaps He withheld from you and gave you. When He opens the door of understanding in withholding, withholding becomes the very essence of giving.'* [1]

12. Some pains are too great to ignore, push away, or try to accept. Live with them. They will die over time.

13. Look at the universe, look closely, and ponder... Isn't it magnificent? All of it is made for you. Do you still think you are nothing?

14. Do good and move on. Goodness will knock on your door on the darkest night when you thought you were alone.

15. Smile no matter the pain; the storm will pass, the winds will calm, and the sunlight will fill the furthest corner of your heart.

16. Be brave for yourself. Fight valiantly even in your weakness.

---

1   Ahmad Ibn Ata'Allah al-Sakandari

Fight because you have something that others don't, and it will be the tool you fight with until the last breath. And know well that you will triumph.

17. Open your arms and soar.

I AM IN THE ERA OF DAILY GENOCIDES

I open my eyes to sunlight.
I tell myself to get up quickly.
My mind asks, 'why?' I answer, 'there's a final exam,
a quiz, a university project discussion, a Zoom meeting,
a part-time job interview as a student, a family event,
a friend's birthday, shopping, meeting a friend.'
My mind responds in a barely audible whisper,
'A long time has passed, Haia, you are in a new
period.' I ask, 'where am I?'
The scent of tea, the sound of the radio,
my mother approaching. The announcer's voice
'a new massacre in Khan Younis, Al-Mawasi.'
My mind rewinds. Yes, that was a sound louder
than any I had heard before. I woke for a few seconds
thought it was a nightmare and fell back asleep,
illness had taken over me.
Today's radio is the compass in the era of daily genocides
this world has grown accustomed to. I didn't understand.
My mind asked, 'is the shedding of blood permissible
in this world?' Bloodshed, home demolitions, displacement,
hunger, thirst – all internationally forbidden, of course,
outside the borders of Gaza. But in Gaza, everything is allowed
even the killing of children.

THEY CHOOSE VICTORY OR VICTORY

In the farthest corner of the world there are dreamers
who chose freedom within the confines of a prison.
They built their homes from the sweat of their brows
constructed with love and hope amidst pain.
They brought happiness and decided to build a new
generation far from death. Their hearts resemble those
of angels, to the extent that sometimes you'd believe
they are. From the ashes they soar like the phoenix.
Even if all doors were closed in their faces you'd find
them searching for hope's clean window.
They've performed miracles simply by staying alive.
In adversity, they function like a single moving body
where if one part aches the entire body rallies with endurance
and diligence. They are akin to the heroes we read about
in stories forging history through their sacrifices.
They refused to abandon their principles in an unprincipled
time. Their souls were the cost of their nation's flag
peacefully fluttering for a new liberated generation
living safely in their homes. They are people who have
never known the path to despair believing in victory
because they are the rightful owners of both truth and land.
They chose victory or victory.

THE HANDS OF TIME STOP IN MY HOMELAND

Life   pulses   beyond the borders   day by day   the gap

widens   life roars outside   death surrounds   from every

direction   you run with your family   your tent

                    in all directions   people outside

chase   dreams   you race   against

time   to secure water   food   for the day   while they run

to offer to keep   warm   the ones who kill us

              you stop running   only to realise

a year has passed   without a home   a university without work

                              without

a city   without life   you realise time is

stealing you away   while you stand helpless   unable to move you

stop   to watch your life   dreams vanish

          before you   powerless   the hands   of time   outside

keep turning   travellers pass by   and journeys continue

              you remain   frozen

in halted time   death tightens its grip

sometimes   you escape   other times

you're struck   under fire   your crime?

                    Your crime?

16

THIS IS MY SISTER

This is my sister Amani and my brother Abdullah,
on New Year's Eve, laughing at videos they captured
during the genocide. Amani started talking to us
about my father, about his love and his generosity.
These moments which may seem ordinary
are the most precious. They are the warmth
that shields from the life's coldness.
You have taught me so much, dear sister.
You've shown me how to never let despair
find its way to my heart. Despite everything
you completed your master's degree, volunteered
to teach children at a school, and cared for Aleen
amidst the horrors of this genocide. On your birthday
I celebrate the light you brought into my world.
I want you to know your presence is not just a blessing
it's a sanctuary.

THE IDEA OF RETURNING REVIVED OUR SPIRITS

My mother was listening to Al Jazeera. The news came that the occupation army withdrew from Khan Younis. At first, we didn't believe it, then the news spread and the movement in the street increased. Everyone went back to their homes. When my aunt called and told us she was going, she encouraged me and my sisters to go back to our home. 'The idea of returning revived our spirits.' We walked half the way, then managed to get a ride until we reached the heart of the city. When I arrived, I stood in front of the streets and the destruction. Is this a nightmare or did I get lost? Did I enter a world of ghosts? It resembles everything except my home. There is a neighbourhood completely burnt, another demolished and another bombed. There are bodies in the streets and people trying to identify them. There are body parts. As for the streets, they are just white ashes, as soon as you walk on them they scatter and you become completely white. My house, the only memory left to us from my father, where he spent his youth, working hard for his family and building the house with the sweat of his brow, where we laughed growing up, and celebrated our big and small achievements. Everything was destroyed. And my brother's house, who recently got married, my dear brother, it's good you travelled so you wouldn't see the destruction. I won't forget how hard you worked building your home over the years, gathering furniture for your new family. It's not just our house or my brother's house, but all the houses in the city were demolished. I didn't cry. I couldn't cry or even know what to cry for. Should I cry for the house, or for my future, or for the country, or the sight of our situation?

DAUGHTER OF THE SEA

I climb to the rooftop where my earth
meets the sea with my journal in hand
a cup of guava leaves after my mother
swore this morning she wouldn't care
for me if I fell ill.

She saw my clothes soaked my teeth
chattering like branches in a storm
I burned with a stubborn desire
a fierce urge to break free from fear
into something more stubborn than me.

I found myself before the raging sea
before dawn the cold was devouring
whispering *if you're going to defy,
don't do it half-heartedly. Don't walk in,
jump!*

In an instant I realised I was in the Arctic
my body trembled but wouldn't surrender
I wished I hadn't defied anyone, I wished
I'd killed that fire in me but I kept swimming
told my body the victim of my defiance, *it's okay*

I swam deeper, a voice behind me broke
my thoughts, *get out you'll drown the sea
is unforgiving!* I answered back *who said
we can't drown on land!* I kept swimming
while the world sat on the shore and watched.

Tonight I can hear the whispers of the wind through olive trees
I strive to protect, the laughter of children mixed with sorrow,
the murmurs of the earth urging me to persevere.

ACKNOWLEDGEMENTS

To my father who rooted freedom within me.

To my mother who embodies the essence of a Palestinian woman – strong, steadfast, unbreakable.

To my brothers and sisters, my refuge in this life.

To my sister Aliya, who taught me to rise each day and carry my name with pride and meaning and to Sunnah Khan for all the support and encouragement she's shown.

To Patricia Ferguson, who embraced me with her humanity when borders and bureaucracy sought to confine me.

To Anthony Anaxagorou, a real man who carried my words as a banner and delivered them to the other side of silence.

To all who read what I've written, this is only the beginning.

If the words touch you may they hold your humanity, not mirror the silence of so much of the world.

I am free. From the sea to the river. No coloniser will silence me. No exile can displace me. No death can kill my cause.

All proceeds from the sale of this pamphlet will go directly to the author. If you would like to make a further contribution to support the poet and her family, you can donate to the GoFundMe campaign accessible at the QR code below, or at the following link: gofund.me/caeb23c2